FAT
(Facts and Tips) *of the*
Land Cookbook

ELIZABETH HENDERSON

PAGE PUBLISHING
Conneaut Lake, PA

First originally published by Page Publishing 2023

ISBN 979-8-88654-791-7 (pbk)
ISBN 979-8-88654-792-4 (digital)

Printed in the United States of America

I dedicate this book to my loving and only daughter, Mauricia Monique Holman, who is the reason I am stronger, wiser, and better, better, and so much better! When I look back over all the things the Lord brought me through, I can see that it was because of your love. It helped me hold on to the horns of salvation and immortality. I never would have made it without your love and the love of God. This cookbook is my imprint here on Earth that I leave to the world, my daughter, and most of all, my precious granddaughter, Monroe Elizabeth Haley.

> And take your father and
> your households, come unto me;
> and I will give you the good of
> the land of Egypt, and ye shall
> eat the fat of the land. (Genesis
> 45:18)

Contents

Introduction

I have written this cookbook at the age of 64/65 during a pandemic crisis. It was birthed to encourage, inspire, and motivate someone who has dreams to share their cooking experiences and think that they are too old or that it is too late to pursue or to do something they have never done before in life. I want to elevate your mind to think the impossible is possible and take your mind and your thoughts to a new level. I want you to speak to yourself, your spirit, and your mind and say, "I believe I can fly. I believe I can reach the sky. I believe I can reach my goal and feed a multitude of souls with motivation." I want you to relish in knowing you can succeed in any accomplishment or achievement and be superior in doing what you believe in and in what others cannot see in you and do not think or expect you to excel in. I hope my book will empower you and give you back the confidence you might have lost as well as the power of cooking more delicious foods to create an environment of more family time together. I pray that your household will enjoy more and use the good, absolute best, finest, and richest of food in this cookbook: *FAT (Facts and Tips) of the Land Cookbook*. I hope and pray my words influence you to become the fearfully and wonderfully made person God intended you to be. Marvelous are His works! This is my book of victory!

Salads, Soups, and Casseroles

The earth brought from vegetation, plants yielding seed after their kind, and trees bearing fruits with seed in hem, after their kind, and God saw that it was good.

—Genesis 1:12

15 Bean Soup

Instructions

1 pkg. Hurst's HamBeens 15 Bean Soup
8 c. water (use bone broth for added flavor)
1 lb. smoked ham hocks (or leftover ham bone with
    some meat on it)
1 large onion (white), diced
1 garlic clove, minced
1 15 oz. can stewed tomatoes
juice from 1 lemon
1 tsp. olive oil
1 tsp. apple cider vinegar
1 tsp. sugar

Directions

Step 1. Soak the beans overnight.
Step 2. In a colander or sieve, rinse the beans thoroughly. Sort and inspect for any unwanted debris and discard.

Step 3. Drain and pour the beans in a slow cooker with 8 cups of stock/water, onion, garlic, and meat or hambone.

Step 4. Stir to combine. Set the slow cooker on high and cook for 5–7 hours then check to make sure the beans are tender. The soup can continue to simmer for several hours and will develop more flavor over time.

Step 5. After the beans are tender, remove the ham bone (leave any ham in the pot) then stir in the can of stewed tomatoes, the ham flavor packet, lemon juice, sugar, and apple cider vinegar.

Step 6. Cook for an additional thirty minutes then keep warm until ready to serve.

Step 7. I recommend serving this with freshly baked corn bread muffins!

Tips

- For even more flavor, use beef or vegetable stock instead of water.
- You can add other vegetables like carrots and celery for even more flavor and nutrients.
- You can also add frozen okra as it cooks quicker.

Fruit Salad

Ingredients

2/3 c. fresh orange juice
1/3 c. fresh lemon juice
1/3 c. packed brown sugar
1/3 tsp. grated lemon zest
1 tsp. vanilla extract
2 c. cubed fresh pineapple
2 c. strawberries, hulled and sliced
3 red apples, peeled and sliced
3 bananas, sliced
2 oranges, peeled and sectioned
1 c. seedless grapes
2 c. blueberries

Directions

Step 1. Bring the orange juice, lemon juice, brown sugar, orange zest, and lemon zest to a boil in a saucepan over medium-high heat. Reduce the heat to medium-low and simmer until slightly thickened (about 5 minutes). Remove the saucepan from the heat and stir in vanilla extract. Set this aside to cool.

Step 2. Layer the fruit in a large clear glass bowl in this order: pineapple, strawberries, apples, bananas, oranges, grapes, and blueberries. Pour the cooled sauce over the fruit. Cover and refrigerate for 3 to 4 hours before serving.

Seafood Salad

Ingredients

1 lb. cooked shrimp
1 lb. Jumbo Lump Crab Meat
6 oz. tuna fish (albacore)
2 boiled eggs
1 celery stalk, finely chopped
1/2 red bell pepper, finely chopped
2 scallions, aka green onion
dill relish
1 c. Hellmann's mayonnaise
1 tsp. freshly squeezed lemon juice or juice from half
    of a fresh lemon
1 tsp. Old Bay Seasoning
crab cake, seasoned
kosher black pepper to taste

Directions

Step 1. In a large bowl, lightly toss the crab meat, shrimp, tuna, eggs, celery, onion, bell pepper, and relish together.

Step 2. In a medium bowl, stir together the mayonnaise, lemon juice, and seasoned crab cake seasoned. Add the dressing to the crab meat and shrimp mixture and stir until just coated. Season with Old Bay Seasoning and pepper to taste. If not using right away, refrigerate until ready to serve.

Step 3. Serve on toasted rolls, crackers, or a bed of lettuce.

Southern Carrot, Pineapple, and Raisin Salad

Ingredients

1 lb. shredded carrots
1 1/4 c. raisins
1/2 c. crush pineapple
2 tbsp. Hellman's Real Mayonnaise (or to your taste)
1 tsp. lemon juice
1/4 tsp. salt

Directions

Step 1. Mix carrots, pineapple, and raisins together in a large bowl.
Step 2. Whisk mayonnaise, lemon juice, and salt together in a small bowl until smooth.
Step 3. Pour lemon juice mixture over carrot mixture and stir until carrots are completely coated.
Step 4. Refrigerate until chilled (at least thirty minutes).

Spanish Salad with Mandarin Orange and Olives

Ingredients

1 can mandarin orange
1 small bag baby spinach leaves
1 small Spanish onion, finely sliced
1/2 c. small black olives, pitted
1/2 c. blanched whole or flaked almonds, toasted
1 tbsp. orange juice
1 tbsp. sherry vinegar
3 tbsp. polyphenol-rich olive oil
a dash of sea salt

Directions

Step 1. Place in a large bowl the spinach, onion, and olives. Mix in the mandarin orange and almonds.
Step 2. Whisk together the orange juice, vinegar, and olive oil and season with sea salt. Pour this over the salad and toss gently.

Spicy Shrimp and Kale Soup

Ingredients

4 tsp. olive oil, divided
1 lb. cooked shrimp (peeled and deveined)
5 garlic cloves, minced
1 bunch kale, trimmed and coarsely chopped
1 c. chopped onion
1 medium sweet red pepper, cut into 3/4-inch pieces
8 c. chicken broth
2 c. fresh mushrooms
1 tsp. chopped fresh basil
3 small organic carrots
1 can okra and stewed tomato
1 bouillon cube
juice of 1 lemon
salt and pepper to taste

Directions

Step 1. Heat oil in a large saucepan over medium-low
heat. Cook and stir mushrooms, onion, carrots,

and garlic in the hot oil until tender (5 to 7 minutes).

Step 2. Pour chicken broth into the saucepan along with the bouillon cube. Add basil. Bring the broth to a boil then reduce the heat to low. Place a cover on the saucepan and let simmer until the basil seasons the broth (about 10 minutes).

Step 3. Stir kale, salt, and pepper into the broth; bring to a boil again, reduce heat to low, and simmer until kale softens, about 10 minutes.

Step 4. Stir in cooked shrimp, okra and tomato, lemon juice into broth; cook about 15 minutes.

Sweet and Spicy Coleslaw

Ingredients

2 lbs. shredded cabbage
4 carrots
1 medium onion
1/2 c. dill relish
1 1/4 c. Hellmann's mayonnaise
1 ½ tsp Nishiki 100% Rice Vinegar
1 c. sugar
1/2 tsp. cayenne pepper
1/2 tsp. ground black pepper
a dash of kosher salt

Directions

Step 1. Peel the carrots and onion and cut into pieces. Toss vegetables, cabbage, carrots, and onion into a large bowl.

Step 2. Prepare the coleslaw dressing by whisking together the mayonnaise, mustard, relish, rice vinegar, sugar, 1 tsp black pepper and the cayenne in a medium bowl. Toss the dressing with the cabbage mixture

Sweet Potato Casserole

Ingredients

Filling.

4 to 6 large sweet potatoes (peeled and cubed)
3 large eggs
1/2 c. raisins
1/2 c. walnuts, chopped
1/2 c. milk
1/4 c. dark brown sugar, packed
1 tsp. pure vanilla extract
1 tsp. cinnamon
1 tsp. nutmeg
a pinch of salt

Topping.

1/2 c. all-purpose flour
1/2 c. brown sugar, packed
1/2 stick (4 tbsp.) unsalted butter, melted
1/4 tsp. kosher salt
3/4 c. chopped walnuts

Special equipment.

a 2-quart baking dish

Directions

Step 1. For the sweet potatoes, add 1 3/4 pounds of peeled and cubed sweet potatoes to a large pot of salted water. Bring this to a boil over high heat, then lower the heat to a simmer and cook until the potatoes are very tender (15 to 20 minutes). Drain and cool. Mash the sweet potatoes.

Step 2. For the filling, preheat the oven to 350 degrees Fahrenheit. Butter a 2-quart baking dish.

Step 3. Whisk together the butter, mashed sweet potatoes, milk, brown sugar, vanilla, cinnamon, nutmeg, salt, and eggs in a large bowl. Stir in the raisins and nuts. Transfer to the prepared baking dish.

Step 4. For the topping: Combine the flour, brown sugar, butter and salt in a medium bowl until moist and the mixture clumps together. Stir in the pecans. Spread the mixture over the top of the sweet potatoes in an even layer. Bake until mostly set in the center and golden on top (25 to 30) minutes. Serve hot.

Yellowfin Tuna Casserole

Ingredients

1 12-ounce pkg. egg noodles
1/4 c. onion, chopped
1 can evaporated milk
2 cup Cheddar cheese, shredded
1 cup green peas (frozen)
2 5-ounce cans yellowfin tuna
2 10.75-ounce can condensed cream of mushroom
    soup
1 cup Utz potato chips, crushed
paprika

Directions

Step 1. In a large pot with boiling salted water, cook
    the egg noodles until tender. Drain.
Step 2. In a large bowl, combine the cooked egg noodles,
    cream of mushroom soup, evaporated milk, tuna,
    cheese, green peas, and chopped onion. Pour into
    a greased 1.5-quart casserole dish. Sprinkle on
    top crumbled potato chips and paprika.

Starches

*Every moving thing that is alive shall be food for
you, I give all to you, as I gave the green plant.*

—Genesis 9:3

Brown and Wild Rice Medley

Ingredients

1 pkg. (6.7 ounces) mushroom-flavored brown and
　　wild rice mix
1 large white onion, chopped
1 cup fresh green beans, cut (1/2-inch pieces)
1 tbsp. flaxseed oil
1 c. sliced fresh mushrooms
2 medium carrots, shredded
1/4 c. chopped sweet red pepper
1/4 c. slivered almonds, toasted

Directions

Step 1. In a large saucepan, cook the rice mix according to package directions, omitting butter.
Step 2. Meanwhile, in a large nonstick skillet, sauté onion and green beans in the flaxseed oil for two minutes. Add the mushrooms, carrots, and pepper. Sauté for 3 to 5 minutes longer or until the vegetables are tender. Add the vegetables and almonds to the cooked rice. Stir until blended.

Nutrition facts

A 3/4-cup serving of this dish is equal to 135 calories, 4 grams of fat (0 saturated fat), 0 cholesterol, 325 milligrams of sodium, 23 grams of carbohydrates (3 grams of sugar and 2 grams of fiber), and 4 grams of protein.

Southern-Style BBQ Baked Beans and Smoked or Jimmy Dean Sausage

Ingredients

2 (28 oz. each) cans Bush's Baked Beans
1 medium-sized sweet onion, chopped finely
1 small bell pepper, chopped finely
1 c. barbeque sauce
1/2 c. light brown sugar
1/4 c. ketchup
1 tbsp. yellow mustard
1 1b. smoked or Jimmy Dean sausage

Directions

Step 1. Cook the sausage, onion, and bell pepper together in a large skillet.

Step 2. Meanwhile, in a large bowl, combine both cans of beans, brown sugar, BBQ sauce, and mustard. Mix well.

Step 3. Add the drained sausage to the beans.

Step 4. Transfer the mixture into a 9 × 13" casserole dish and bake at 350 degrees Fahrenheit for about 30 minutes.

Vegetables

Better is a dish of vegetables where love is;
than a fattened ox served with hatred.

—Proverbs 15:17

Stir-Fried Kale, Cabbage, and Bok Choy

Ingredients

12 oz. uncooked bok choy (trimmed)
8 oz. uncooked kale (tough stems removed)
1/2 small cabbage
2 tsp. canola oil
3 large garlic cloves, sliced
1 1/2 tsp. fresh ginger root, grated
1 1/2 soy sauce
1/4 tsp. dark sesame oil
a dash of crushed red pepper flakes

Directions

Step 1. Cut the bok choy crosswise about 1/2 inch to 3/4 inch thick (you'll get about 6 cups). Set aside. Slice kale leaves crosswise about 1 inch thick (you'll get about 8 cups). Set aside.

Step 2. Heat the oil in a large, deep, nonstick wok over medium heat. Add the garlic and ginger then cook, stirring frequently, until fragrant (about 1 minute).

Step 3. Add the bok choy and kale. Stir-fry them over medium-high heat until the vegetables are tender (about 6 minutes). Remove the wok from the heat and stir in soy sauce, sesame oil, and pepper flakes. This recipe yields about 1 cup per serving.

Notes

Have leftover chicken, beef, or pork? Add it to the stir-fry and heat through for an easy main dish.

Pickled Jalapeños
and Red Onions

Ingredients

3 jalapeños, sliced
1 large red onion, sliced into half moons
1 c. apple cider vinegar
1/4 orange juice
3 tbsp. lime juice
1 tsp. sugar
1 tsp. kosher salt
1 c. water

Directions

Step 1. Put the jalapeños and red onion in a 16-ounce widemouthed Mason jar.

Step 2. In a small saucepan, combine the vinegar, orange juice, lime juice, sugar, salt, and water. Bring the mixture to a boil, stirring until the sugar and salt are dissolved.

Step 3. Pour the hot liquid over the veggies in the jar, screw on the lid, and set aside. When it has cooled to room temperature, transfer the jar to the fridge to chill for a minimum of an hour, which will allow the vegetables to pickle. The pickles will last in the fridge for 3 to 4 days. Serve them on pulled pork and BBQ sandwiches.

Sautéed Cabbage and Kale

Ingredients

1 small head of cabbage, chopped (1 lb. or about 2.26 c.)
1 lb. fresh kale, steamed and roughly chopped
3 tbsp. olive oil
1/2 c. onion, chopped
2 garlic cloves, very finely chopped
1 tbsp. butter
1 bunch scallions (4 to 5 stalks), chopped
salt
freshly ground black pepper

Directions

Step 1. Heat the olive oil in a large pan over medium heat. Add the chopped onion and cook for 3 to 5 minutes or until it begins to soften.
Step 2. Add the garlic and continue cooking just until fragrant (about 1 minute longer).

Step 3. Add about 1/3 of the chopped cabbage. Season with a pinch of salt and cook until wilted and reduced in bulk.

Step 4. Repeat with the other two batches of cabbage, being sure to season with bit more salt each time.

Step 5. Continue cooking, stirring often, until the cabbage is caramelized and golden in color (15 to 18 minutes).

Step 6. Add the butter and a few grinds of black pepper, then adjust the salt to taste.

Step 7. Add the kale and continue cooking until it's wilted and tender (3 to 4 minutes), then add the scallions and cook until slightly softened but still bright green. Transfer to a serving dish.

Spring Vegetable Medley

Ingredients

6 oz. trimmed baby carrots, peeled
1 lb. asparagus, trimmed and cut into 4-inch lengths
8 oz. sugar snap peas, stringed
1 large fennel bulb, thinly sliced
2 tbsp. olive oil
1 tbsp. fresh tarragon, chopped
3 c. vegetable stock
salt
pepper

Directions

Step 1. Bring the vegetable stock to a boil.
Step 2. Add the carrots and let cook for 1 minute.
Step 3. Add the asparagus, fennel, and peas. Cook until all vegetables are crisp-tender (about 2 minutes longer).
Step 4. Drain vegetables and return them to the pot. Add the oil and tarragon and toss to coat. Season to taste with salt and pepper.

Tips

- Substitute vegetables can be added, such as broccoli, cauliflower, etc.

Summer Squash Sauté

Ingredients

1 1/2 tbsp. olive oil
1 large yellow squash, chopped
1 large zucchini, chopped
3 garlic cloves, chopped
1 c. grape tomatoes
kosher salt to taste
a dash of crushed red pepper
2 tbsp. shredded Parmesan cheese (optional)
basil vinaigrette for drizzling (optional)

Directions

Step 1. Heat the olive oil in large skillet on medium-high heat. Add the yellow squash and zucchini and cook for 3 minutes, stirring occasionally.

Step 2. Add in the garlic and tomatoes and cook for 2 to 3 minutes, gently stirring, or until the vegetables are crisp-tender and the tomatoes are about ready to burst.

Step 3. Season with salt and crushed red pepper. Sprinkle with Parmesan cheese, if using, and drizzle with basil vinaigrette, if using. Serve immediately.

Tips

- Other vegetables can be added or substituted, such as eggplant, onion, carrots, etc.

Meats

And God said, Behold, I have given you every herb bearing seed, which (is) upon the face of all the earth, and every tree, in the which (is) the fruit of a tree yielding seed; to you it shall be for meat.

—Genesis 1:29–31

Crawfish Étouffée

Ingredients

1 stick (1/4 lb.) butter
2 c. onions, chopped
1 c. celery, chopped
1/2 c. bell peppers, chopped
1 lb. peeled crawfish tails (or shrimp)
2 bay leaves
1 tbsp. flour
1 c. water
1 tsp. salt
1/4 tsp. cayenne pepper
2 tbsp. parsley, chopped
3 tbsp. green onions, chopped

Directions

Step 1. Melt the butter in a large skillet over medium-high heat. Add the onions, celery, and bell peppers and sauté until they turn soft and golden (10 to 12 minutes).

Step 2. Add the crawfish and bay leaves. Reduce the heat to medium and cook, stirring occasionally, for about 10 to 12 minutes.

Step 3. Dissolve the flour in the water. Add this to the crawfish mixture and season with salt and cayenne pepper. Stir until the mixture thickens (about 4 minutes). Add the parsley and green onions and cook for about 2 minutes.

Step 4. Remove the bay leaves and serve.

Homemade DC's Mumbo Sauce Chicken Wings

Ingredients

Mumbo sauce.

1 (6 oz.) can tomato paste
1 c. BBQ sauce
2/3 c. ketchup
1 c. pineapple juice
1/2 c. orange juice
1 c. distilled white vinegar
1 lemon, juiced
1/4 cup honey
2 tbsp. soy sauce
1/1/2 tbsp. freshly grated or powdered ginger
1 tsp. cayenne pepper

Wings.

canola/peanut oil
flour
4 lbs. chicken wings, separated

2 tbsp. your favorite wing rub

Directions

Step 1. Place the tomato paste, ketchup, and sugar in a saucepan. Pour in pineapple juice, orange juice, white vinegar, lemon juice, BBQ sauce, and honey into the pan. Add soy sauce, grated ginger, and cayenne pepper. Whisk together thoroughly.

Step 2. Place pan over medium-high heat. As soon as mixture stats to bubble, reduce heat to medium-low and simmer, whisking occasionally, until mixture has thickened slightly, about 10 minutes.

Step 3. Remove pan from heat; allow to cool about 10 minutes or so. Pour sauce through a fine strainer to eliminate solids.

Directions for wings in a deep fryer. Heat the canola or peanut oil to 375 degrees Fahrenheit. Coat the wings with rub and flour, shake of the excess, and drop them into a deep fryer. Fry 8–10 wings at a time, 5–6 minutes per side or until the chicken is done. Transfer to paper-towel-lined plate to drain excess oil. Transfer the cooked wings to a bowl and add the sauce from earlier, tossing gently to coat.

Directions for wings in an oven. Preheat oven to 450 degrees Fahrenheit. Place the wings into a resealable bag or container. Add the mumbo sauce. Seal the bag and shake well to coat. Let the wings marinate for 1–3 hours. Line a large baking sheet with aluminum foil. Spread the wings out on the baking sheet and bake for 20 minutes. Flip the wings and bake them for another 15–20 minutes or until the chicken is done. Transfer the cooked wings to a bowl and add the sauce from earlier. Toss gently to coat.

Mississippi Pot Roast

Ingredients

3–5 lb. chuck roast
flour
oil (to sear)
1 packet Hidden Valley Original Ranch Seasoning,
　　Salad Dressing & Recipe Mix
1 stick unsalted butter
1/2 cup beef broth
8 whole peperoncino peppers

Directions

Step 1. Season the chuck roast generously with salt
and pepper. Rub enough flour over the roast to
evenly coat the surface.

Step 2. In a large skillet, warm the oil over high heat
until very hot but not smoking. Sear the roast
until browned and crusty on all sides (about 10
minutes total).

Step 3. Place the roast in the pot of a slow cooker. Pour
the beef broth around the roast. Then sprinkle

with seasoning mix, top with butter, and scatter
peperoncino over and around the roast.

Step 4. Cover the slow cooker and set it on low heat
for 7 to 8 hours. When ready, shred the meat,
mixing with the sauce in the slow cooker.

Tips

- Serve this over bread, egg noodles, or
mashed potatoes.

Fun fact

The original recipe for what is known as
Mississippi pot roast first began to cause a stir in
the early 2000s when Robin Chapman of Ripley,
Mississippi, started riffing on a chuck roast recipe she
remembered from her aunt.

Old-Fashioned Meat Loaf

Ingredients

Meat loaf.

1 1/2 lbs. beef chuck or ground beef
1 c. tomato juice
3/4 c. quick oats
1 egg, beaten
2 tbsp. brown sugar
1/4 c. onion, chopped
1 1/2 tsp. salt
1/4 tsp. black pepper

Sauce.

1 1/2 c. brown sugar
1/2 tsp. garlic powder
1 c. water
2 tbsp. Worcestershire sauce
1 c. ketchup

Directions

Step 1. Combine all ingredients of the meat loaf and
mix well. Do the same for the sauce.

Step 2. Form the meat loaf mixture into small loaves
and place in a small-to-medium loaf pan.

Step 3. Pour sauce over top of the loaves and bake
at 350 degrees Fahrenheit for 75 minutes. Let
stand for 5 minutes before serving.

Panko Fried Chicken

Ingredients

2 lbs. bone-in chicken drumsticks or thighs, with
    skin
kosher or sea salt to taste
freshly cracked black pepper to taste
2 large eggs
2 c. panko bread crumbs
vegetable oil (for frying)

Directions

Step 1. Rinse the chicken drumsticks/thighs and pat
    them dry. Season them with salt and pepper to
    taste and set aside.
Step 2. In a large bowl, beat the eggs and set aside. In
    another large bowl, add the panko and set aside.
Step 3. Coat a piece of chicken in egg and dredge it
    in the panko, shaking off any excess afterward.
    Set the coated pieces aside and repeat with the
    remaining chicken.

Step 4. Heat 1 inch of oil to 375 degrees Fahrenheit in a large frying pan or Dutch oven.

Step 5. Working in small batches, gently place the chicken in the hot oil and fry on both sides until crispy and cooked through (10 to 15 minutes on each side).

Tips

- The baked-in-the-oven version is quick, tasty, and healthier, and it still lets you indulge in crispy goodness! Brush a sheet pan with some oil and spread the chicken out onto the sheet pan. Bake the chicken for 12 to 15 minutes or until chicken is done and golden.
- For better results, roll the chicken in flour before the eggs. The eggs will stick to the chicken better.
- You can also substitute the meat in this recipe to do panko fried fish.
- Enjoy chicken with your favorite condiment or sauce!

Pickled Pig's Feet Souse

Ingredients

6 pig's feet
dill pickles, chopped
1 tbsp. whole cloves
1 tbsp. peppercorns
1 tbsp. salt
2 tbsp. lime/lemon juice (freshly squeezed)
2 large garlic cloves, mashed
1 scallion head, chopped
3 c. distilled white vinegar
2–3 c. stock (reserved from draining the cooked pig's feet)

Directions

Step 1. Scrape and clean the pig's feet well and put them into a pot to boil in enough salt water to cover. Let simmer for approximately 4 hours or until the meat will separate from the bones. Remove the feet from pot, allow them to cool, and chop the meat.

Step 2. Mix the stock in which meat was cooked with vinegar, lemon/lime juice, scallion head, salt, peppercorns, and spices. Bring this mixture to a boil and keep it boiling for 30 minutes. Strain the liquid to remove spices.

Step 3. Place the pieces of meat and chopped dill pickles in a flat dish or stone jar and pour some liquid over it (leave at least 2 cups of stock left in the pot). Chill in refrigerator until perfectly cold. Slice and serve.

Sloppy Joe

Ingredients

2 1/2 lbs. beef chuck
1 large green bell pepper, diced
1/2 large onion, diced
1 c. water
1 1/2 c. ketchup
5 garlic cloves, minced
hot sauce
Worcestershire sauce
salt
freshly ground black pepper
2 tbsp. packed brown sugar
2 tsp. chili powder, or as needed
1 tsp. dry mustard
1/2 tsp. red pepper flakes, or as needed
2 tbsp. butter, softened
8 Kaiser rolls

Directions

Step 1. Brown the meat in a large pot over medium-high heat. Drain off the fat.

Step 2. Add in the green bell peppers and onions. Stir the mixture and then add the water, the ketchup, and the garlic. Stir it around to combine, then add the brown sugar, chili powder, dry mustard, red pepper flakes, hot sauce, Worcestershire sauce, salt (to taste), and pepper (to taste). Stir to combine, and then cover and simmer over medium-low heat for about 20 minutes.

Step 3. To serve, spread the rolls with the butter and brown them on a skillet. Spoon a good amount of the meat mixture onto the bottom roll and then top with the other half. Serve with chips or coleslaw, or just enjoy it by itself.

Tips

- Prepare chips or coleslaw for serving if desired.

Slow Cooker Carolina Pulled Pork BBQ

Ingredients

1 (5 lbs.) bone-in pork shoulder roast or pork butt
1 tbsp. salt
ground black pepper
1/2 c. apple cider vinegar
2 tbsp. brown sugar
1 1/2 tbsp. cayenne pepper
2 tsp. crushed red pepper flakes
1 tbsp. garlic powder
1 tbsp. paprika powder
1 tbsp. cumin powder
2 tsp. onion powder
4 tsp. Worcestershire sauce
1 lemon

Directions

Step 1. Place the pork shoulder into a slow cooker and season it with salt and pepper. Pour the vinegar around the pork. Cover and cook on low heat for 12 hours. The pork should easily pull apart into strands.

Step 2. Remove the pork from the slow cooker and discard any bones. Strain out the liquid and save 2 cups. Discard any extra. Shred the pork using tongs or two forks and return it to the slow cooker.

Step 3. Stir the brown sugar, garlic powder, cumin powder, onion powder, paprika powder, Worcestershire sauce, lemon, hot pepper sauce, cayenne pepper, and crushed red pepper flakes into the reserved sauce.

Step 4. Mix the sauce into the pork in the slow cooker. Cover and keep on the low setting until serving time.

Southern Fried Cabbage and Sausage

Ingredients

1 small green cabbage, chopped
3 tbsp. polyphenol-rich olive oil
1 small white onion, chopped
1/2 lb. smoked sausage, sliced (Hillshire Farm)
1 (15 oz.) can Hunt's Diced Tomatoes
1/4 tsp. garlic, minced
1/4 tsp. Morton Season-All salt
black pepper to taste

Directions

Step 1. In a large nonstick skillet, precook the sliced sausage for about 5 minutes to render some of the fat.

Step 2. Remove the sausage from the skillet and drain on paper towels. Set aside. Wipe the skillet clean.

Step 3. In the same skillet, pour in olive oil then add cabbage and onion. Cook and stir on medium-high heat for about 10 minutes or until the cabbage begins to wither. Add the remaining ingredients and the sausage.

Step 4. Cover the skillet and cook for another 10 minutes. Uncover, and finish cooking until cabbage is desired tenderness and most liquid has been reduced and ready to serve.

Stuffed Cabbage Rolls

Ingredients

Rolls.

12 cabbage leaves
1 c. cooked brown rice
1/4 c. finely chopped onion
1 large egg, lightly beaten
1/4 c. fat-free milk
1/2 tsp. salt
1/4 tsp. pepper
1 lb. lean ground beef (90% lean)

Sauce.

1 can (8 oz.) tomato sauce
1 tbsp. brown sugar
1 tbsp. lemon juice
1 tsp. Worcestershire sauce

Directions

Step 1. In batches, cook the cabbage leaves in boiling water for 3 to 5 minutes or until they become crisp-tender. Drain then cool slightly. Trim the thick vein from the bottom of each cabbage leaf by making a *V*-shaped cut.

Step 2. In a large bowl, combine rice, onion, egg, milk, salt, and pepper. Add beef. Mix lightly but thoroughly. Place about 1/4 cup of the beef mixture on each cabbage leaf. Pull together the cut edges of the leaf to overlap then fold over the filling. Fold in the sides and roll it up.

Step 3. Place six rolls in a 4- or 5-quart slow cooker, seam side down. In a bowl, mix the sauce ingredients and pour half of the sauce over the cabbage rolls. Top with the remaining rolls and sauce. Cook, covered, on low heat for 6 to 8 hours or until a thermometer inserted in the beef reads 160 degrees Fahrenheit and the cabbage is tender.

Desserts

Why spend money on what is not bread, and your labor on what does not satisfy? Listen, listen to me, and eat what is good, and you will delight in the richest of fare.

—Isaiah 55:2

Apple Brown Betty

Ingredients

4 c. soft white bread crumbs (about 6 slices of bread)
1/3 c. butter, melted
1 c. packed brown sugar
1 tbsp. ground cinnamon
4 large green (Granny Smith) apples, peeled and cut
    into 1/4-inch slices
1 c. apple cider

Directions

Step 1. Heat the oven to 350 degrees Fahrenheit. Lightly spray a 2-quart casserole with cooking spray.

Step 2. In medium bowl, stir together bread crumbs and melted butter. In small bowl, mix the brown sugar and cinnamon.

Step 3. Place half of the apple slices in the casserole and sprinkle with half of the brown sugar mixture and half of the bread crumb mixture. Repeat the layers. Pour the apple cider over top.

Step 4. Bake for 45 to 55 minutes or until the apples are tender and the topping has browned. Serve warm.

Peanut Butter-Oatmeal Pecan Cookies

Ingredients

2 c. quick-cooking oats
2 c. flour
2 sticks butter (unsalted, room temperature)
2 eggs (room temperature)
1 1/2 c. chocolate chips
1 1/2 c. pecans (diced)
1 c. peanut butter (creamy)
1 c. brown sugar
1 c. white sugar
1 tbsp. vanilla
1 tsp. baking powder
1 tsp cinnamon
1/4 tsp salt

Directions

Step 1. Preheat oven to 350 degrees Fahrenheit. While the oven preheats, beat the butter and sugar together in a mixer until creamy. Add eggs one at a time, beating for about 20 seconds between each addition.

Step 2. Add peanut butter and vanilla then beat well.

Step 3. Mix flour, salt, baking powder, and cinnamon together in a bowl, reserving 1 tablespoon to toss chocolate chips in prior to adding.

Step 4. Add flour to butter-sugar mixture in 3 batches, beating 20 seconds between each batch and scraping down the sides of the mixer.

Step 5. Add the oats to the mixer and beat for 20 seconds. Toss chocolate chips and pecans with the reserved flour and add them to mixer. Beat for about 20 seconds.

Step 6. Chill the dough in the refrigerator for at least 30 minutes.

Step 7. Using a rounded tablespoon to form the dough into balls. Use a fork to make a crisscross on each ball, flattening them.

Step 8. Bake the cookies at 350 degrees Fahrenheit for 12 to 13 minutes. Allow them to cool for a few minutes before serving.

Southern Sweet Potato Cake

Ingredients

Cake.

4 large eggs
2 c. sugar
2 c. canola oil
2 tsp. vanilla extract
2 c. all-purpose flour
2 tsp. baking soda
2 tsp. ground cinnamon
1/2 tsp. ground ginger
1/2 tsp. ground allspice
1/2 tsp. salt
3 c. shredded and peeled sweet potatoes (about 2 medium-sized ones)
1 c. finely chopped walnuts

Frosting.

1 pkg. (8 oz.) cream cheese, softened
1/2 c. butter, softened

1 tsp. vanilla extract

2 c. confectioner's sugar

Directions

Step 1. Preheat oven to 350 degrees Fahrenheit. Grease a 13 × 9-inch baking pan.

Step 2. In a large bowl, beat the eggs, sugar, oil, and vanilla until well blended. In another bowl, whisk flour, baking soda, spices, and salt together. Gradually beat this into the egg mixture. Stir in the sweet potatoes and walnuts.

Step 3. Transfer the mixture to a prepared pan. Bake until a toothpick inserted in the center comes out clean (about 40 to 45 minutes). Cool completely in pan on a wire rack.

Step 4. In a small bowl, beat the cream cheese, butter, and vanilla until blended. Gradually beat in the confectioner's sugar until smooth. Spread over cooled cake. Refrigerate the leftovers.

Breads and Muffins

*Take wheat and barley, beans and lentils, millet
and spelt, put them in a storage jar and use
them to make bread for yourself. You are to eat
it during the 390 days you lie on your side.*

—Ezekiel 4:9

Banana Nut Muffins

Ingredients

1/2 c. mashed banana
2 c. flour
1/2 c. chopped walnuts
1 tsp. baking powder
1/2 tsp. salt
1/4 tsp. baking soda
3/4 c. brown sugar
1 stick butter (melted)
2 eggs
1/2 c. sour cream

Directions

Step 1. Mix 2 cups of flour, 1/2 cup of chopped walnuts, 1 teaspoon of baking powder, 1/2 teaspoon of salt, and 1/4 teaspoon of baking soda.
Step 2. Whisk 3/4 cup of brown sugar, 1 stick of melted butter, 1/2 cup each of mashed banana

and sour cream, and 2 eggs; fold this into the
flour mixture.

Step 3. Divide the batter among 12 prepared muffin
cups. Bake for 20 to 25 minutes.

Gingerbread Muffins

Ingredients

2 c. flour
2 tbsp. cocoa powder
1 tbsp. ground ginger
1 tsp. baking soda
1/2 tsp. salt
1 stick butter (melted)
1/2 c. sugar
1/2 c. molasses
1/4 c. milk
2 eggs

Directions

Step 1. Mix 2 cups of flour, 2 tablespoons of cocoa powder, 1 tablespoon of ground ginger, 1 teaspoon of baking soda, and 1/2 teaspoon of salt.

Step 2. Whisk 1 stick of melted butter, 1/2 cup each of sugar and molasses, 1/4 cup of milk, and 2 eggs; fold into the flour mixture.

Step 3. Divide the batter among 12 prepared muffin cups; bake for 20 to 25 minutes.

Jalapeño-Cheddar
Corn Bread Muffins

Servings: 12 muffins
Total time: 30 minutes

Ingredients

1 1/4 c. all-purpose flour, spooned into a measuring
    cup and leveled off
3/4 cup yellow cornmeal
1 large jalapeño pepper
1/4 c. plus 2 tbsp. sugar
1 tbsp. baking powder
1 tsp. salt
2 large eggs
2 tbsp. honey
3/4 c. milk (preferably whole, but low-fat works too)
1 stick (1/2 c.) unsalted butter, melted and cooled
4 oz. (1 cup) sharp Cheddar cheese, grated

Directions

Step 1. Preheat the oven to 350 degrees Fahrenheit. Line a muffin pan with paper liners or spray with nonstick cooking spray. (I prefer to use a nonstick cooking spray so the muffins get nice and crisp on the edges.)

Step 2. In a medium bowl, break up the eggs with a whisk. Whisk in the honey and then the milk. Set aside.

Step 3. In a large bowl, whisk together the flour, cornmeal, sugar, baking powder, and salt. Add the milk mixture and the melted butter to the dry ingredients. Whisk until just blended. Do not overmix; it's okay if there are a few lumps.

Step 4. Spoon the batter evenly into the prepared muffin pan, filling each cup about ¾ full. Bake for 30 minutes, or until the tops are set and golden. (Note that the muffins will not dome.) Cool the muffins for a few minutes in the pan, then serve warm.

Tips

- If you'd prefer to make this as cornbread rather than muffins, spray an 8-inch square pan with non-stick cooking spray and bake at 350 degrees for 25 to 30 minutes.

- *Freezer-friendly instructions:* Corn bread muffins taste best when served right out of the oven but can be frozen in an airtight container or sealable plastic bag for up to 3 months. Thaw for 3 for 4 hours on the countertop before serving. To reheat, wrap them in aluminum foil and warm them in a 350-degree-Fahrenheit oven until hot. Alternatively, heat the muffins in the microwave at 50 percent power for 30 to 45 seconds or until just hot; do not over-heat, or muffins will get tough.

- *Substitute using green onion, cracklings, or cream corn.*

Pumpkin Walnut Muffins

Ingredients

1 1/2 c. all-purpose flour
1 tsp. baking soda
2 tsp. pumpkin pie spice
1/4 tsp. salt
1 c. granulated sugar
1/4 c. light brown sugar, packed
1 c. canned pumpkin puree
1/2 c. buttermilk
1/4 c. Star Extra Light Olive Oil (plus more for oiling
    the muffin pan)
1 egg
3/4 c. chopped walnuts

Directions

Step 1. Preheat the oven to 375 degrees Fahrenheit.
    In large bowl, whisk together the flour with the
    baking soda, pie spice, and salt.

Step 2. In another bowl, combine sugar, pumpkin puree, buttermilk, oil, and egg. Whisk until well blended.

Step 3. Stir in the dry ingredients just until completely incorporated. Fold in the pecans. Spoon the batter equally into 12 oiled muffin cups and bake for 20 to 25 minutes or until the muffins spring back when lightly touched in the center. Remove the muffins from the pan and let cool on a wire rack. Serve warm or at room temperature.

Sauces

For the Lord your God is bringing you into a good land—a land with brooks, streams, and deep springs gushing out into the valleys and hills; a land with wheat and barley, vines and fig trees, pomegranates, olive oil and honey; a land where bread will not be scarce and you will lack nothing.

—Deuteronomy 8:7–9

Homemade BBQ Sauce

Ingredients

2 6-oz. cans tomato paste
1/2 c. ketchup
1/2 c. apple cider vinegar
1 small sweet onion, chopped finely
1/2 c. brown sugar
3 tbsp. honey
2 tbsp. Worcestershire sauce
juice of 1 lemon
3 tsp. smoked paprika
1 tsp. dry mustard
1 tsp. garlic powder
1 tsp. kosher salt
1 tsp. black pepper
hot sauce to taste

Directions

Step 1. Combine all ingredients in a medium-sized saucepan.

Step 2. Place the saucepan over medium-high heat on your stove top or grill, keeping an eye on the sauce and stirring regularly.

Step 3. Once the sauce begins to simmer, drop the heat to low.

Step 4. Allow the sauce to thicken to your desired consistency, stirring every now and then.

Step 5. Serve with your favorite grilled, back, or fried meats and enjoy.

Homemade Red Hot Sauce

Ingredients

12 very ripe red jalapeños (about 10 oz.) or a mix
    of fresh chilies such as habanero, serrano, and
    Fresno
1 1/2 tbsp. minced garlic
1/2 c. diced onions
2 tbsp. kosher salt
1 tsp. vegetable oil
2 c. water
1 1/2 c. distilled white vinegar

Directions

Step 1. Pulse the chilies, garlic, onions, and kosher
    salt in a food processor until you have a rough
    puree. Transfer this to a 1-quart glass jar, loosely
    cover, and let sit at room temperature overnight.
Step 2. Add the vinegar, stir, and loosely cover. Let sit
    at room temperature for 1 to 7 days. The longer
    you let it stand, the more the flavor develops.

Step 3. Pour the mixture into a food processor or
   blender and puree until smooth. Store in the
   refrigerator up to 4 to 6 months.
Note: The hot sauce may separate. This is normal;
   shake before use.

Homemade Strawberry Vinaigrette Dressing

Ingredients

1 pkg. (16 oz.) frozen unsweetened strawberries, thawed
1 c. lemon juice
1/4 c. sugar
2 tbsp. apple cider vinegar
2 tbsp. polyphenol-rich olive oil
1/8 tsp. poppy seeds

Directions

Step 1. Place the strawberries in a blender; cover and process until pureed. Add the lemon juice and sugar; cover and process until blended.

Step 2. While processing, gradually add the vinegar and oil in a steady stream; process until thickened. Stir in the poppy seeds. Transfer the dressing to a large bowl or jar; cover and store in the refrigerator.

Polyphenol-Rich Olive Oil and Balsamic Vinaigrette Dressing

Ingredients

1/2 c. polyphenol-rich olive oil
1/4 c. balsamic vinaigrette
2 tbsp. raw honey
1 tsp. Dijon mustard
1 garlic clove, minced
1 tsp. sea salt
1 tsp. pepper

Directions

Step 1. Combine the olive oil, balsamic vinaigrette, honey, Dijon mustard, garlic, salt, and black pepper together in a glass jar with a lid. Replace the lid on the jar and shake vigorously until thoroughly combined.

Vinegar-Based BBQ Sauce (Carolina Style)

Ingredients

2 c. apple cider vinegar
1 c. ketchup
1/2 c. brown sugar
1/4 c. hot sauce
2 tbsp. chili powder
2 tbsp. whole peppercorn
1 tbsp. salt
1 tbsp. chili pepper flakes
1 tsp. dry mustard

Directions

Step 1. Place all the ingredients in a pan. Cook this on a stove top at medium heat. Bring it to a boil. Whisk together until the sugar and salt are completely dissolved.

Step 2. Remove the saucepan from the heat. Cool the sauce to room temperature. Pour the sauce into a jar or squeeze bottle and let it rest in the refrigerator for 1 day before using.

Drinks

Whether therefore ye eat, or drink, or whatsoever ye do, do all to the glory of God.

—1 Corinthians 10:31

Holiday Iced Tea Punch

Servings: 15–20
Total time: 15 minutes

Ingredients

2 qt. Fresh Arizona Sweet Tea
1 can (46 oz.) pineapple juice
1 can (12 ounce) orange juice
1 can (12 ounce) lemonade
1 c. ginger Ale

Directions

Mix all the ingredients together and pour over ice cubes into a tea dispenser.

Tips

- Any of your favorite sweet teas can be used as a substitute. Also, you can add limeade instead of lemonade and cranberry juice instead of orange Juice for a different flavor.

Homemade Sweet Lemonade Iced Tea

Ingredients

3 c. water
4 tea bags (Lipton)
1 can (12 oz.) frozen lemonade concentrate
2 c. cold water
8 c. ice cubes
8 thin slices lemon

Directions

Step 1. In a large saucepan, bring 3 cups of water to a boil. Remove it from the heat. Add the tea bags. Let sit for 10 minutes to steep.

Step 2. Remove and discard the tea bags. Add the lemonade concentrate and cold water. Stir to blend. Pour the liquid into a serving pitcher. Add ice cubes and lemon slices.

- Add sugar, slices of lime, or fresh mint leaves to your desire.

Watermelon Punch

Ingredients

6 c. watermelon juice
2 c. pineapple juice
1 can (12 oz.) frozen raspberry juice blend
1 small can (6 oz.) frozen orange juice concentrate
1/4 c. lemon juice

Directions

Just combine all ingredients in a large jar or pitcher and serve chilled over crushed ice.

Note: To make watermelon juice, pick up one 10-lb. oblong watermelon. Process small chunks of watermelon (with seeds removed) in a blender or food processor until they turn to liquid.

Tips

- Make more than you need for this punch, freeze the extra in ice cube trays, and use the watermelon cube to chill the punch.

(You can also use watermelon juice instead of water when preparing frozen lemonade or limeade)

Appendix A

Aromatherapy

Fragrance	Helps Promote	Helps Relieve
Black pepper	Quitting smoking	Anxiety
Ginger	Sharpness	Fatigue
Cinnamon	Concentration/ memory/mental sharpness	Fatigue/ memory loss
Orange	Optimism/peace/ happiness confidence	Anger/depression/ fear/ stress/irritability
Peppermint	Clear thinking/ concentration sharp memory	Fatigue
Grapefruit	Confidence/ peace/happiness	Depression/fear
Lemon	Peace/happiness/ memory/ concentration	Fear/fatigue/ indecision confusion
Vanilla	Relaxation	Depression

Tangerine	Calmness	Stress
Thyme	Energy/courage/drive/confidence	Fear
Basil	Clear thinking/calmness	Fatigue/anxiety
Rosemary	Clarity/memory concentration	Fatigue/nervous tension

Appendix B

DIY Home Remedies

Kitchen cleaning spray

Pour 32 ounces of water into a large spray bottle. Add 3 tablespoons of baking soda and 15 drops of orange oil. Shake well and use it for your kitchen counter, fridge, and even pantry. Your kitchen will have a lovely citrus scent.

Glass cleaner

Mix the following ingredients in a spray bottle then shake well before each use (spray this on glass surfaces and wipe clean).

- 1/2 cup white vinegar
- 1/2 cup rubbing alcohol
- 10 drops lemon

Bakeware cleaner

To clean cookie sheets or muffins pans with baked-on residue, mix and apply this recipe while wearing cleaning gloves. Mix the following ingredients in a bowl until a paste is formed (add more baking soda to thicken, if needed). Use a cleaning cloth to work the paste into the bakeware. Scrub in a circular motion and rinse thoroughly. Reapply and repeat as needed until bakeware is clean and shiny.

- 1/4 cup baking soda
- 1/4 cup hydrogen peroxide (3% solution)
- 10 drops pink grapefruit essential oil

First aid spray

Using a tea tree oil spray for minor cuts and scrapes from sharp knives and utensils while cooking in the kitchen helps prevent infection and promote healing. Combine the following ingredients in a small spray bottle, shake well before each use, spray on the affected area, and allow to air-dry.

- 2 ounces purified water
- 20 drops tea tree essential oil

Pest repellent spray

Peppermint oil naturally repels mosquitos, spiders, garden pests, and mice. To keep pests out of your home and away from your plants, pantry, and kitchen, make a peppermint oil spray by putting 8 to 12 ounces of water in a spray bottle and adding in 10 to 15 drops of peppermint oil. Shake well and spray around door frames, windows, and near (not on) plants.

Mosquito repellent

Combine the following ingredients in a clean spray bottle and shake well before use. Apply this to clothing or surrounding areas.

- 1/2 cup witch hazel
- 1/2 cup distilled water
- 10 drops lemongrass essential oil

Fruit fly and gnat relief

Combine 2 tablespoons of red wine vinegar with 1/2 teaspoon of Dawn dishwashing liquid in a small glass. Stir gently to prevent bubbles. Cover this with plastic wrap. With a skewer, poke a few holes in it. The flies can get in but cannot get out.

Acknowledgments

Special thanks to my pastor, Bishop Linwood Elijah Dillard, for his encouragement and his visionary and spiritual leadership. I began to pursue my cookbook during the period when Pastor Dillard was preaching and teaching a series on Joshua's leadership. The book of Joshua in the Bible is the book of victory. I learned through Bishop Dillard's teaching that we are created to rule, govern, control, master, manage, and lead our environments. We are created to dominate, not to be dominated. All human beings were designed and born to use their unique gifts and talents in the world. This is my time to give myself to the world. It is an honor and a blessing to be under this young man's powerful leadership.

I win.

About the Author

Elizabeth Henderson was born and raised in the Delta of Greenwood, Mississippi. She relocated and lived in an area of Washington, DC, for over forty-five years. Before retiring in 2018 from the General Services Administration (a federal government agency) as a supervisor, contract officer, and team leader, she earned her bachelor's degree in business administration from Strayer University and an MBA from Averett University. She now resides in Memphis, Tennessee. At the age of sixty-six, her motto is "You don't have to retire after retirement; there's still work to do." She is the proud mother of one awesome and beautiful daughter—Mauricia Monique Holman—and the grandmother of one beautiful precious granddaughter: Monroe Elizabeth Haley.

Her accomplishments include the following:

- having a poem published in *Great Poems of the Western World* (2005) by Lavender Aurora (poetry editor) (Famouspoets.com) (her poem can be found on page 185)
- Dale Carnegie graduate (May 30, 2007)
- USDA Executive Leadership Program graduate school (May 23, 2008)
- Federal Acquisition Certification in Contracting Level III (August 21, 2009)
- contracting officer, warrant up to $10,000,00 (August 3, 2010)
- 1999 GSA Regional Administration Award for Seamless Customer Service
- 2005 GSA National Capital Region Customer Relations Award
- GSA Service Award (completion of twenty-five years)